Jala and the Wolves

Written by Marti Dumas

Illustrated by Garyl Araneta

Cover Art by Marie Muravski

ISBN-10: 1-943169-00-4
ISBN-13: 978-1-943169-00-9

For Jala, who inspires me.

Contents

Chapter 1

A Not So Ordinary Girl

Once there was a little girl. Jala was her name. By all accounts she lived an ordinary life. She had a mother and a father, a sister and a brother, a bunk bed, a fish named Oscar, and seemingly thousands of tiny toys that liked to lurk about and lodge themselves in her mother's feet. Her life was wrapped in a cloak of love so warm and snug that Jala often had difficulty seeing past the end of her nose.

That's not to say that Jala was blind. She could see perfectly well. But as is often the case for 6 year-olds who are well-loved and well-cared for, Jala had plenty of time to get bogged down in details that less fortunate children would happily overlook. Her hair, for instance. It was long and tangled easily and took hours to be combed out properly. Just the thought of getting her hair combed was enough to worry Jala to tears and she lived in constant fear of it, like a boogie monster waiting to gobble her up. She much preferred wearing her hair in its natural state—standing wild and free, twisting in all directions—but even then her mother insisted on smoothing down the edges and that was a bother, too.

Then there was her brother. She loved him. She knew she did. But every time he got praised for doing two-year-old things in his two-year-old way she couldn't help wishing that she could get so much attention for blowing her own nose, or saying "love" instead of "wuv," too.

But her brother and the imminent threat of hair-combings were nothing compared to the food. Jala was ALWAYS hungry. Always. No matter how many meals she ate, she always seemed to have room for another. Her parents would give her firsts and often gave her seconds, but whenever she asked for thirds all she got were sharps looks and explanations about how she is a girl, not a hobbit, and there is a difference between being hungry and just wanting more food to eat. This frustrated Jala to no end. That and the fact that her parents refused to let her eat her meals from a dog-dish on the floor, nor did they allow her to pretend to be a dog while eating from a dish on the table. (That last part they'd only let her do for two weeks before they made the "No Animals in the Kitchen" rule.)

What Jala didn't know, and what no one could tell her, was that she was exceedingly special. To be sure, everyone knew she was wonderful. She was kind and caring and deeply loving. Everyone knew she was smart. She had been reading everything in sight since she was 3 and gobbled up facts about animals that stumped most grown-ups. Everyone even knew she was beautiful. With her gorgeous face, dark, almond shaped-eyes and long slender legs she was as elegant and lovely as any Degas ballerina. Those things made her special, but no one, including Jala, knew quite how special she was until the day before the feast.

Chapter 2

Breakfast

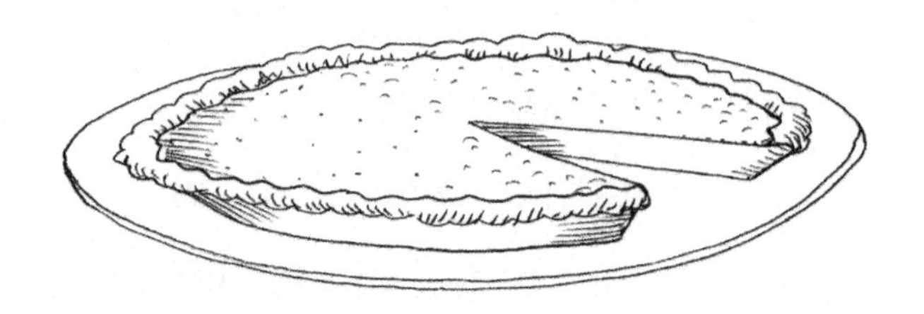

The day before Thanksgiving dawned bright and cool. It never got truly cold where Jala lived, so the cool days brought her almost as much joy as a snowfall. It meant she could wear her favorite lollipop-striped tights without her legs getting all sweaty and itchy. It also meant she could watch her warm breath hanging in the air, a favorite pastime of hers.

Cool weather also meant that it was finally autumn and the Thanksgiving feast might be as close as the calendar promised. True, her teacher had been talking about Pilgrims and Native Americans and cornucopias for the last couple weeks, but teachers talked about a lot of things a lot. So until she walked down the long hallway that ran the length of their house and stepped out on the front porch in her bare feet to check the weather for herself, she couldn't be certain Thanksgiving was truly near. But there it was: a cool breeze and the icy stab of cold concrete on the soles of her feet.

It was autumn alright, even in New Orleans, and for Jala that meant only one thing. Pie. Bean pie to be exact. Don't go turning up your nose at it, either. Bean pie is perfectly delicious. If you're the kind of person who likes pumpkin pie or sweet potato pie, bean pie will be right up your alley. Jala had been dreaming about its sweet, cinnamon-y goodness ever since the previous Thanksgiving, which is odd when you know how much of a carnivore Jala usually was.

Jala's family was not exactly vegetarian, but her parents had waited to introduce meat to her and her brother until they were each two years old. At almost 3 her brother still refused the stuff, scraping the breading off chicken with his bottom teeth and leaving the flesh to be thrown away. Not Jala. When she was almost 3 she would eat as much meat as her parents allowed, sucking the bones when she could get away with it. She loved meat so much that once she even asked for a bite of her father's lamb in a Lebanese restaurant. Her father, not really wanting to share, had reminded her that lambs were baby sheep and that sheep were her favorite animals at the time. Undaunted despite her love of sheep and creatures of all kinds, Jala took a bite anyway and uttered the following rather irreverent noise in response:

"Mmmm-baaaa."

"Well," her parents shrugged, "she's not a vegetarian," and continued with their meal.

Jala was not one of those kids who hated vegetables. Even so, bean pie was one of the few plant-y things that held such a high place in Jala's carnivorous heart. Needless to say, the Thanksgiving feast with its whole roasted turkey, chicken and sausage gumbo, and the promise of at least 2 (maybe 3) bean pies made Jala's heart flutter in what could only be called a dance of joy. Meat followed by pie? How much better could it get?

So after slipping on her candy pink tights and a dress of an entirely different color, Jala made her way to the kitchen to see if the Thanksgiving feast was already in bloom.

Sure enough her mother was there, standing at the stove making what looked suspiciously like cream of wheat and not pie at all. There wasn't even a stray bean on the floor to indicate that a bean pie might be in the oven, but did that deter Jala? Not in the least. In her mind cool day=Thanksgiving=pie. Simple math. All she had to do was find it.

As soon as she entered the kitchen area her keen nose picked up the faint smell of cinnamon hanging in the air. It was the slightest smell. Hardly anything to notice at all. Another, less fortunate child would have paid it no mind at all because she would have been worrying about something truly sad like how to stay safe, or how to get warm, or how to find a place to sleep. But Jala, being a fortunate child, didn't have to worry about such things and therefore had the freedom to smell the smell in the first place and the audacity to hope that it came from a bean pie, perhaps cooling somewhere she could not see it. Jala was very good at hoping for things even if she wasn't always very good at telling people what she hoped for.

She approached cautiously, sliding on stockinged feet like a predator stalking its prey. Asking mothers pesky questions while they are cooking is not always a good idea. Sometimes it gets you sent away without your question answered, or sent to your room without any books to read. If Jala had truly taken a moment to think about it she might have even worried that she might be told she couldn't have any bean pie at all. But the thought of the pie was so alluring that that last bit didn't occur to her and she stalked a little closer.

"Good morning, mama," she said, testing the waters.

Her mother looked a bit tired, but glanced up from the cutting board with a warm smile and responded,

"Good morning, baby." She was cutting Gala apples into thin, half-moon slices before plopping them into the cream of wheat, so she only glanced at Jala before returning to her cutting. "Did you sleep well?" her mother asked without looking up again.

Definitely cinnamon, Jala thought. And butter. And a sweetness. Was it brown sugar? Perhaps agave? She wasn't certain which, but there was definitely a sweetness in the air. Jala was so distracted trying to untangle these lovely smells that she forgot to answer her mother's question entirely and said this instead: "I'm hungry."

Jala wasn't really hungry. It was morning and she hadn't eaten yet so for her that meant breakfast—hopefully a special breakfast. Her mother was silent for a few moments, and when a grown-up who likes to talk as much as Jala's mother is silent that's never a good sign. Jala, too tangled up in hope to recognize this, repeated herself.

"I'm hungry, mama," she said again. That boldly hopeful part of her envisioned the scene playing out like this:

Jala's mama: You're hungry baby?

Jala: [nodding eagerly] Yes, mama!

Jala's mama: I can't let my baby be hungry, not even for a moment! This cream of wheat is not ready yet, so would you take… [Reaching behind her and producing a plate of bean pie with a flourish] this instead?

Jala: [nodding eagerly and clapping hands

with excitement] Oh, yes! It's what I've always hoped for! Thank you, mama!

Jala's mama: In fact, bean pie is so healthy for you, you could have it for breakfast EVERY DAY if you like. Would you like that, Jala...?

Unfortunately for Jala that is not how the scene played out at all because she had managed to strike upon three of her mother's most deeply held pet peeves at once.

Pet Peeve #1: Stating the obvious. For Jala's mother, Jala saying she was hungry was like jumping into a swimming pool and then saying you're wet. Duh. You didn't need to say that.

Pet Peeve #2: Children who have never missed a meal acting like there is the real possibility they might not be fed. Since there are plenty of children in the world who must *actually* worry about where their next meals will come from, Jala's mother felt it was conceited and spoiled for well-fed children to do this.

Pet Peeve #3: People (especially Jala) ignoring her questions.

By the time Jala could see the annoyance brewing in her mother's eyes, it was too late to turn back. She had already said it. Twice. So the scene actually played out like this.

Jala's mama: Jala, did you notice that I am already making breakfast?

Jala: [nods]

Jala's mama: Do you think that telling me you're hungry will make the breakfast be ready any faster? Or were you thinking that I might feed everyone else breakfast, but forget to feed you?

Jala: [standing silently, unsure of what to say]

Jala's mama: When the cream of wheat is ready, I will call you. Go back to your room, Jala.

Jala never even had a chance to say that what she really wanted for breakfast was bean pie (which was probably for the best since this would have struck pet peeve #4: asking for junk food before you have eaten any healthy food) because her mother gave her such a withering look that all she could do was retreat to her room.

Once there, Jala checked to see if the coast was clear. Her mother had not told her she couldn't read while she waited for breakfast, but she also hadn't said she could. Jala didn't want to take any chances so after looking over her shoulder to see if the hallway was empty, she closed her eyes and put one ear up so she could really listen. Besides her sister snoring from the bottom bunk and the clink of the spoon in the cream of wheat pot, the house was silent and the coast seemed to be clear.

When she opened her eyes again that's when Jala noticed there were two things out of the ordinary in her room. The first thing was that one of her favorite books, The Wolves in the Wall by Neil Gaiman, was on the dollhouse rug that lay in front of her bunk bed. She didn't remember it being there when she had climbed down the bunk bed ladder that morning or when she came back to get dressed, but there it was on the floor.

Her sister was still sleeping. She had just gotten in from her other home in Georgia late the night before, so she would probably be sleeping for a while. Besides, being 12 years old she was an unlikely candidate for taking a picture book off the shelf and dumping it on the floor. That was more her baby brother's style. But the house was way too quiet to say he was awake, so Jala just assumed The Wolves in the Wall had been on the floor the whole time.

Glancing over her shoulder to make sure there was still no one watching her from the hallway, Jala snatched the book up and turned to head over to her comfy reading corner to enjoy it.

That was when she noticed the second thing. Her reading corner was very different than it had been. This she was certain of. The cushy red ottoman had been replaced with a sky blue bean bag chair, and in front of it hanging in a most improbable place beneath the windowsill was a looking glass.

Chapter 3

The Looking Glass

Jala could tell the looking glass was magical the moment she saw it, and that did not surprise her one bit. Why? Why, her mother was magical, of course. That had been obvious to Jala for years. How else could her mother always know what she was thinking before she said it? And how else could her mother have produced so many snacks, juice boxes, warm sweaters and first aid supplies at exactly the right moment? Her mother had done magical things so many times that Jala had ceased to be amazed by it.

No doubt about it, this mirror was definitely her mother's handiwork. After all, slipping into her room to make it lovelier while Jala was on the front porch checking the weather was exactly the kind of thing her magical mother would do. So far from being alarmed by the presence of this mirror, Jala was eager to test it out. If her mother put it here it must be safe and besides, Jala and her mother had read Alice's Adventures in Wonderland and Through the Looking

Glass... **twice**, making Jala something of an expert on such matters.

The mirror was perfectly firm to the touch so, having no white rabbits to follow, Jala sat down on the conveniently placed bean bag and gazed into the mirror pondering various ways to make it work. All Skippyjon Jones had to do was bounce on his big boy bed to make himself (he was a Siamese cat) look like a Chihuahua in the mirror and begin his adventures. But Skippyjon was only pretending and that was just a fantasy book. This was real life.

When Jala looked into the mirror, all she could see was her regular face surrounded by messy, morning hair. This was true even when she was bouncing. Clearly getting to the magic in this mirror took more than just looking at it or jumping around.

After a few more minutes of puzzling Jala decided not worry about it. Undoubtedly her mother would tell her the trick of the mirror at breakfast. Then they could go on a mother-daughter adventure together before anyone else had even woken up. All she had to do was wait to be called and not get in trouble in the meantime.

The thought of having a private adventure with her mother was so delightful that Jala almost forgot how hungry she thought she was and nestled herself deeper into the sky-blue bean bag chair to read The Wolves in the Walls and wait for her mother to call her.

Jala loved wolves. She had started out playing at monkeys, then progressed through several different species of the cat family before she had finally settled into the canines. It started with sheepdogs, but it wasn't long before sheepdogs led to wolves. There was something about the howling that appealed to her. And the moon. The moon? Yes. The moon. Over the top of her book she imagined she could see the moon hanging full and round in the mirror. But it wasn't her imagination. The fullest, roundest moon she had ever seen hung over a rocky ledge, the base of which was surrounded by a deep pine forest.

There was a white wolf standing on that ledge. The wolf was standing so still that Jala had almost convinced herself that the whole scene was a picture, when, with a sudden flash, the wolf turned to look at her. Their gazes locked. The only thing Jala could think of was how much the white wolf's eyes looked like her sister's hazel ones. But there was another flash and the wolf's eyes went from hazel to the darkest, truest brown there was and Jala felt herself falling and not knowing when she would stop.

Chapter 4

Jala and the Wolf

If she didn't know she was a wolf before she landed, she knew as soon as her feet hit the ground. Four feet. Paws, really. They were beautifully padded so that landing on that rocky ledge felt more like landing on the rubber mulch in her school playground. The world around her was alive with smells. She could tell who and what was around her without even turning her head. Behind her was rock. The scent of goat and turkeys and other prey came drifting from overhead. Below her were pine trees and fresh water, insects, squirrels, deer, and another wolf. She did not need to look down to see him. She knew he was there. Knew he was gazing up at her, waiting for an answer.

His name was Milo. At least that's what it smelled like to her. Wait. Not smelled like. That would be weird. Seemed like. His name seemed like it was Milo. He was young with fur the nutty brown color of toasted almonds. They had sent him because, of all the young wolves, Milo was the most fearless traveler and had ventured far from the pack many times.

When Jala finally looked down at him she looked straight in his eyes as her mother had taught her to, and did not look away. Milo whimpered then. It was a tiny sound. The kind a puppy would make. That sound told her he was worried and afraid. That was all the sound said, but his smell was telling her much more. She knew that the rest of his pack was several hours' walk away. She knew that if she did not return to them with him he felt certain they would die. She knew that he was worried that he had displeased her in some way. The question was how did she know all that from a scent on the breeze? The expression on his face and the way he held his tail told her a lot, but besides that little whimper, Milo hadn't made so much as a sound. Was she reading his mind or were the smells really talking to her?

Here was another puzzle for her to tease out. At least she had figured out how to use the mirror on her own. The mirror! Thinking of the mirror made Jala suddenly very conscious of her new body. She leaned back, stretching out her haunches. Then she pounced forward suddenly, the way tigers do on nature videos, and landed lightly on all four paws. Standing on four legs was nothing like crawling on your hands and knees. As much as Jala liked to pretend to be a dog, it did make your knees hurt after a while. And no matter how much you pretended to run, you couldn't really run when you crawled like that. Having four legs was another thing entirely.

Padding over to the edge of the ledge, Jala felt as though nothing could knock her over while she was on her four legs. On two legs she had never noticed how each leg depended on the other for balance, but on four legs it was impossible to miss. It only took eight steps for her to feel graceful, ten to feel powerful, and by the thirteenth she felt positively magical enough to leap off the ledge toward the wolf who smelled like Milo waiting for her below.

Up close to him she knew even more. She circled him once, sniffing the whole while the way she had seen dogs greet each other in the park. The one she called Milo stood still through the examination as she sniffed him and the air. At first the smells were a jumble of meaning. The pack was hungry. They had prayed for her to come. Hunting. Beauty. Water. Sickness. Hunger again. Slowly the smells began to disentangle themselves and Jala began to realize that Milo was talking to her—not with grunts or human voices—the way dogs truly do: with smells.

"We have been waiting for you, Jala," Milo began. "Our old one knew how to call you, but she was too weak to come herself. She sent me instead to call you back to us. We need you."

He looked up at her then. She realized he had been avoiding her eyes, but the look in his eyes was all submission and pleading. Jala nodded in response. It was a human gesture, but he seemed to understand.

"There is a stream up ahead with clear, cold water. We can drink there then start our journey." He snatched another look at Jala's eyes before adding, "If it pleases you."

Another nod from Jala sent Milo bounding towards the forest with her following close behind. Running in this body was the closest Jala would ever get to flying. She closed her eyes with every leap to feel the way the air rustled through her fur and opened them again to watch the moment her front feet landed. When they got to the edge of the forest Milo slowed down. He could run among the trees if they were familiar to him, but he did not know this wood. Their gallop slowed to a walk and Jala drew herself up next to him so that they were walking side by side.

"The stream is just ahead," he told her.

"I can hear it," she thought, "and smell it, too." The water made a tinkling sound, almost like wind chimes, with an equally lovely smell that propelled her forward so that she found herself racing the last of the distance through the trees. All those years of jumping over sponges in her Saturday morning ballet class had made her more agile than she knew. She leaped from place to place in a continuous motion, avoiding brambles and roots and low-hanging branches without even having to think.

Milo was cautious at first, but he soon followed her winding path through the trees, albeit at a slower pace. By the time he caught up with Jala she had already drunk deeply from the stream and was standing by a large puddle near the bank that was leftover from a recent rainstorm. Milo drank his fill, and then went to join her.

Jala could hear Milo's soft panting and the light tread of his paws approaching her before his reflection appeared in the pool beside hers. His face was a soft, reddish brown ringed with a collar of white, where hers was snow-white with tiny flecks of silver, black, and gray. His eyes were amber, with flecks of green and brown like her sister's eyes. Her eyes were so dark brown that they almost seemed black. They were her own human eyes, and seeing them there was something of a relief. It made her know that she was still herself somewhere underneath this beautiful mantle of fur. That was comforting somehow.

What she couldn't see in the reflecting pool was her legs. They were long—longer than most wolf legs by two or three inches—so that even though Milo's body was a bit larger than hers, their heads rested at about the same height. Having long legs was nothing new to Jala. She had been born with long legs. They came in handy for climbing trees and in and out of grocery carts. So if she could have seen her long, beautiful legs, she would not have remarked on their length at all. What would have been most appealing about her new legs besides their strength and balance was the markings that covered them.

She caught Milo looking at her reflection, and held his gaze there. He started to look away, as if he had been caught doing something naughty, but soon collected himself to look back at her.

"You're staring at me," she tried to say, but all that came out was a low rumble in her throat that Milo did not understand. You're not a girl, she reminded herself. At least not now. You're a wolf. Wolves don't talk, they communicate. The word communicate was one of her mother's favorite words. As a human girl Jala often communicated with her actions rather than with words. Sometimes this was okay. For example, throwing your arms around someone rather than saying, "Thank you," or "I love you," was usually received well.

Unfortunately, Jala's way of communicating with her body instead of with her words had gotten her in a lot of trouble, too. For example, in Kindergarten when she attempted to communicate that she didn't want to leave the reading center by kicking, flailing, and crying, that had gotten her two weeks without dessert, which wasn't exactly what she had been looking for.

Jala took a deep breath and tried again. This time she imagined what it felt like to say what she was trying to say and, to her delight, it worked.

"You're staring at me," she said again. She thought/felt the words more than said them. It worked. She knew Milo had understood her because he immediately looked away.

"You stare at me; then you're scared to

look at me. Are all wolves wishy-washy like that?"

"Forgive me," Milo began, "It's just… you're an alpha and I… I've never seen a wolf with eyes like night before."

It was true that her eyes were as dark as night, but Jala was uncertain about the alpha part. "How do you know I'm an alpha?" she asked.

"I don't kn…it's just that I was sent to perform the ritual and make the sacrifice to call forth a new alpha to help us in our time of trouble. I found the great wolf in the sky and ate the last of the dark berries that grew in the brambles at the base of the big rock and tried to connect the stars in my mind just like Dace taught me so that it would look like a true wolf and not just points of light. Then night turned to morning and there you were—the great wolf brought to earth just as Dace knew you would be." Milo communicated this to her in a rush of scents and facial expressions that made her know he was relieved to be able to finally able to tell it to someone. Even though it hadn't been that long since it happened, seeing a wolf appear from the sky was probably a big deal for him so it was understandable that he was eager to talk about it. Whether or not she had actually come from a constellation was a whole different thing entirely.

Jala knew all about constellations. The one he was talking about was called the Great Dog, but it made sense that a wolf would call it the Great Wolf instead. She also knew how hard it was to connect the dots on stars to make them look like the pictures they are supposed to be and she was impressed that Milo had been able to do it without a grown-up around to help. She didn't have the heart to tell him that she was only a girl from New Orleans who got sucked into a mirror and not the Great Dog come to life at all.

"Is Dace a wolf? Is she your alpha female? Why didn't she come do this herself?"

Milo made a snorting noise that was

unmistakably wolf laughter. “Dace is a wolf. Of course she is a wolf! What else would she be? Do you think I would take orders from a squirrel? She was the alpha female in her prime, but that was many winters ago. She is the only wise one left, so when Kyra, our last alpha female, was stricken with the sickness, Dace cared for her as best she could and then stepped into her place when she died. Sort of. But Dace is too old to truly be the alpha female. That is one of the reasons she sent me to find you.”

“What about your alpha male? Is he dead, too?”

Milo hesitated a moment before drawing

himself up to his full height and saying, "I am the alpha male." With his head raised proud and high, he did look like the alpha male…when he was looking at her. "I can range the farthest, I am the strongest, the other males follow my lead, and this will be my third winter."

His third winter? That meant he was almost full grown. If he were human he would be off in college like Jala's cousin Logan. But Logan was just a teenager, really. Sure, she was as tall as a grown-up, but in most other ways she seemed just like all the rest of the kids. Logan's mother still cooked her meals for her and bought her clothes just like Jala's mother did. And here Milo was preparing to be in charge of a whole pack of wolves. Jala couldn't help but feel sorry for him.

"I'm ready," Milo told her, nuzzling her a bit so she would look back at him. There was more meaning in his look, but it was not something Jala could understand yet, so she let it pass.

"If you're the alpha male, then why did you look away whenever I looked at you? That's something omega's do." Jala didn't know everything about being a wolf, but she knew a lot. She had been gathering bits of information about wolves from nature magazines and animal encyclopedias ever since she finished learning all the sheep dog commands. Alpha males and females were sometimes called dominant pairs. That meant that BOTH of them were leaders. Why would one leader have trouble looking another leader in the eye? It didn't make sense.

"It's your eyes," he said.

"I know, I know." Jala felt a bit exasperated. "They're like night. You said that already. Is nighttime scary for wolves, or something?"

"No. Nighttime is beautiful for wolves."

"Great," she responded. "So you won't have any more trouble looking me in the eye then, right?"

Milo looked sheepish then, which is pretty funny when you remember that he is a wolf. "It's not just your eyes, though. It's your markings. Your leg markings. When we reach the pack I won't be the only one staring at you, so you should probably get used to it."

Jala looked down at her legs which is amazingly difficult to do if you are a wolf. She had to lean back on her haunches to see her forelegs, then curl her body up to catch glimpses of her hind legs. Most wolves have at least some variation in color, but typically the fur on their legs is very similar to the fur on their bodies. Jala's fur was different. Her legs were covered with silver rings. Each ring was surrounded by the thinnest band of black at the top and the bottom making the silver stand out even more distinctively against the white of her fur. In fact, the markings strongly resembled the stripes on her lollipop tights, but her lollipop tights were not nearly so cool. Milo was right. If she had seen a wolf with markings like these she would have stared, too.

She started to tell him as much when her ears perked up involuntarily. That faint crunching sound was different from all the other sounds in the forest. It was the unmistakable crunch of hoof on pine needles. A light sniff of the air told her her instinct was correct. Deer.

Chapter 5

The Hunt

Deer. A deer!

A hunger coursed through Jala's veins like she had never known before. She had no time to think. Her body took over. The forest was a blur of green and brown and early morning light. Her legs automatically began to slow as the scent got stronger. The scent of the deer had grown so strong and luscious that she thought her hunger might make her burst.

She consciously slowed her steps even more and began to focus on moving as silently as possible. The deer was close enough to see, now. It was a yearling buck carelessly far from his family. If he saw them, or heard them, or smelled them he would bolt. And from this distance they might not be able to catch him.

Milo drew up alongside Jala. They exchanged a quick look and Jala knew he knew exactly what she was thinking. She turned to head northwest to approach the buck from the north while Milo was to continue on their mostly eastward course. He would remain hidden while she chased the deer toward him. With any luck the deer would be so flustered that he would run right into their trap.

The plan worked. The young buck was confused and frightened and ran exactly the way a lamb would when being herded by a sheep dog. Milo ran toward them at just the right moment and the split second it took the deer to realize that his pursuer was not hunting alone was just enough time for Jala and Milo to simultaneously change course, effectively encircling the deer.

Milo was the one who went for the kill.

Jala was glad that he had. The chase was the most thrilling thing she had ever experienced, but the human in her would have hesitated to kill the beast. Jala, for whom meat came from a grocery store, might have thought about what to do next, and her hesitation might have been just enough time for the deer to escape. Milo spared her all that by lunging forward and biting the beast around its throat. The deer kicked and thrashed for a long while before finally lying still.

Her immense hunger soon overcame any guilt Jala may have felt about the deer. Jala and Milo gorged themselves, and for the first time in her life Jala felt truly full. She and Milo lay side by side near what remained of the carcass, licking blood from their muzzles and feeling generally satisfied.

It was Milo who had the idea to bring the remnants of the deer back to the rest of the pack. Jala agreed, so they dragged the deer carcass for several hours until the smell of home and safety surrounded them. It was the smell of the wolf pack. Her pack.

Chapter 6

Dace

She greeted them as they approached. Her coat was almost entirely black, but not yet thick enough for the coming winter. She was thin, but her eyes with their swirls of amber and grey seemed to hold all the wisdom of the world. This was Dace, the wolf who had taught Milo enough magic to fetch Jala to this world. Strangely, she was just as Jala had expected.

Milo, who had been dragging the deer, dropped it and ran up to her full of nuzzles and excited whimpers like a cub. Dace returned his affection without breaking her decorum. She watched Jala approach from afar.

Jala, who could sense Dace's age and wisdom even from a distance, thought it would be best to approach her with a gift. Clutching a deer hoof in her mouth, she trotted up to Dace at a dignified pace and lay the carcass at her feet.

Dace had no trouble looking into Jala's eyes, but it was Milo she addressed first.

"I see you have found her."

"Yes," Milo replied, regaining a bit of his own decorum. "I have. Everything was just as you said it would be. You read the signs well."

"Too well, I fear. The needles said she would be young, but this one is too young for our purposes. We need a female who will help strengthen our numbers so that the pack will thrive again come spring."

"I caught a deer," Jala said by way of an answer.

"I know you did, my dear," Dace responded in a smell so gentle and loving that it almost felt as though it came from her own mother. Then, as if realizing she had been rude, Dace leaned down and carefully tore a mouthful of deer away from the carcass, getting only the tiniest flecks of blood on her muzzle which she promptly licked away.

"I can catch more," Jala added. There was nothing more annoying than grown-ups doubting her ability. Hadn't she caught a deer within a couple of hours of becoming a wolf? Surely she could catch more.

"Deer are scarce. They had a hard summer, too. Most of them have moved on. The pack should have followed them, but we were in no condition to do so. Come. I will show you."

Dace turned to walk away and it was then that Jala noticed the unevenness of her gait. She walked with a limp, but more than that, she walked with the deliberate slowness of one who was sick and hungry. But if she was hungry, why didn't she eat more of the deer Jala and Milo had brought?

Jala soon found out why. They reached a small clearing surrounded by tufts of high grass. There were lots of bushes that made great shelters and hiding spaces for the hungry cubs who were everywhere. There must have been at least twenty of them poking their noses out cautiously and crouching down behind particularly tall clumps of grass. So many cubs in one place meant this must be the rendez-vous.

Jala had read about this, too. It was a place where cubs went when they were too old for the den, but too young to hunt well with the elders.

Hiding as they were, it was difficult for Jala to get a good look at them. But gradually they began to come forth. At first Jala thought that it was Dace they were coming out to see. Then she thought it was Milo. But by the way they looked at her, some of them staring blankly with their mouths hanging open, she knew it was her. One by one they came up to her, each one scrawnier than the last. Hunting must be as scarce as Dace said it was.

Being cubs, most of them were just learning

about the hierarchy in the pack. They had established a hierarchy amongst themselves as soon as they were big enough to venture outside the den and start wrestling around. The adult hierarchy was still new to them. This meant that most of them were not intimidated by the mere fact that Jala was an alpha. They were staring at her because she was so different. Her long legs with their exotic markings and her dark eyes probably made her frightening and strange to these cubs.

Dace could read Jala's feelings and body language much better than Milo could. Not knowing this, Jala was surprised when Dace responded. "They are not frightened of you. They are in awe of you. You are the most beautiful wolf any of them have ever seen and you smell of a fresh kill."

Azaza, who was bold for her age, stepped forward first. Her fur was the darkest, most beautiful brown Jala had ever seen. It was almost like chocolate. And although she was lean, you could tell that she was powerful.

"Are you our new mother?" Azaza asked. "Will you teach us how to hunt?"

Jala snort-chuckled the way humans do when someone says something surprisingly funny while they are drinking hot chocolate. The result was a perfect wolf laugh.

Azaza seemed offended at first, but then Jala told her, “I am much too young to be your mother, but I can teach you how to hunt.”

Chapter 7

Jala's Wolf Pack

All wolves, alpha and omega, needed to hunt to survive, and Jala wasted no time teaching them. Lacking the sponges her ballet teacher used, Jala set up patterns with pine cones and branches for the cubs to use in practicing their leaps and bounds. Those who were already good at leaping like Azaza, a honey-colored cub named Genny, and her brother Jack moved on to stalking. The trio took to stalking quickly and within a few hours had cornered a fat rabbit. Their hunger made them too eager, though, and all three of them leapt for the rabbit at once. In the confusion the rabbit slipped away easily.

"Wolves hunt best in packs," she scolded the group. "You have to work as a team even when you're hungry. You each could have had a share of rabbit but now you have none." But she knew that was easy for her to say. She had a full belly. Most of the cubs looked as if they hadn't had more than a few mouthfuls in the last few weeks. When they had hauled the deer carcass into the rendez-vous, the cubs had scrambled and fought over it so much that it was impossible to stop their disputes until the last bit of marrow had been sucked from the last bone. Besides a few scraps of fur, not a bit of the deer had been wasted.

The cubs were energetic for a few hours after their meager meal, but it wasn't too long before most of them were too tired to continue.

Jala scanned the rendez-vous area looking for Dace. The wise old wolf was curled up on a small, grassy mound. Jala thought she remembered her sitting proudly upright, watching the cubs as they trained. It seemed that Dace had run out of energy, too.

"Milo! Milo!" Jala called, punctuating her

scent with short howls.

Milo came trotting over from where he had been helping the cubs arrange themselves in sleeping piles. “That was a great lesson,” he began. “You’re such a good teacher. That thing with the pine cones was genius!”

“Thanks,” Jala responded a bit uncertainly. “They did do really well, but they would probably do even better if they had something to eat. When do the adults get back? Are they out hunting for food for the cubs?”

Milo’s head drooped. He took a deep breath and waited a long moment before saying anything. Then Milo howled the most beautiful, painful howl Jala could ever imagine. It was a sound filled with sadness and loss and when the cubs joined in, raising their little heads in their piles to add their voices with Milo's, Jala knew the adults were not coming home.

Jala was so moved by their sorrow that she began to weep. Before she knew it she was curled up in a circle with her tail covering her nose, whimpering as if she had lost her own mother. Then Dace came near, her warm tongue licking Jala on her head and the scruff of her neck in a gesture that cleaned away the sadness while Jala breathed in the story.

It had happened last spring. As usual, the

juveniles had just dispersed to form their own packs while the new cubs and their mothers were still in their dens. Milo was a juvenile then so he had dispersed along with the others. With so many new mouths to feed, the time juveniles normally struck out to make it on their own was before the cubs emerged from their dens in the spring.

The Fathers took turns guarding the den entrances so the mothers could slip out for drinks of water. The wolf pack had been using the same den site for generations back as far as anyone remembered. No one remembered having a fall with no rain and a winter with no snow that was followed by an equally dry spring. The mothers had to range far in search of good water. Eventually there was none left. Desperate, several of the mothers drank from a fetid pool. They got sick first, but soon the sickness spread. Most of the adult wolves were dead within a few days. They kept themselves away from the dens so as not to contaminate the young cubs. That was when Milo had found Dace and two others among the dead. Seeing that he was not sick they begged him to find the young cubs and carry them to a place where they might drink. He made the trip 22 times carrying a cub by the scruff of the neck, once with Dace, half-dragging her when she could no longer walk, and once alone because the other two wolves were already dead.

The scent of the tale hung heavily in the air, coming, as it was, from Dace and Milo, Azaza, Genny, Jack, and all the other cubs. Each had a part to tell. Jala absorbed it and truly understood her purpose. This was her pack. If she did not care for them, no one would. If they were hungry, it was up to her to feed them.

Catching enough deer to fatten up twenty-four hungry wolves before winter was too much for her and Milo alone. Dace would have been an excellent addition to the hunt if she were well, but she wasn't. The cubs were eager to learn, but on a hunt they were more likely to scare the prey away than help catch it. Yet Jala also knew that their only chance to get enough prey was to hunt as a pack—the way wolves hunt best.

Then the wind picked up bringing in the scent of raspberries from the south. All at once Jala knew what to do.

Chapter 8

The Feast

Late autumn raspberries are truly rare. Being from a place where it is warm and things grow all year-round, Jala probably did not realize how rare it was. The rain coming so late in the year had delayed the blooms long enough to produce a perfect crop of raspberries late in the season. They'd be ruined in the first frost, but hopefully they would have served their purpose long before then.

The scent of the berries was so strong and inviting that she didn't know how she hadn't picked it up before as she, Milo, Azaza, Genny, and Jack raced toward the berries. Azaza, Genny, and Jack did an excellent job keeping up with the group, which is remarkable when you consider how much older and larger Milo was. Jala stayed a bit ahead of them the whole time. That was partially so that she could lead the way, but also so that she could work out the last details of her plan.

In the end she decided to keep it simple. Jala arrived several minutes before the rest of the group. There were huge stretches of raspberry bushes in almost every direction. By the time the rest of the group caught up with her Jala's fur and muzzle were stained with splotches of deep pink. The four other wolves pulled up short when they saw her, puzzled.

"It's not gonna work you know," Azaza declared matter-of-factly. "No matter how much you roll around in those berries the deer are still going to smell wolf underneath."

"I'm not trying to mask my scent, Azaza," Jala chuckled. "I'm eating."

The looks on their faces were mixtures of shock and disgust. Raspberries were plants.

Prey ate plants. They were predators. They ate prey. Milo wrinkled up his nose unpleasantly as Jala shook another branch of raspberries with her teeth before lapping the fruit up off the ground with her tongue. Azaza and Jack continued to stare, horrified, while Genny actually started to back away.

"Keep that stuff away from me," Genny's whimper said. "I'm no plant-eater."

Jala thought they were all being ridiculous and whipped out a line her mother often used: "If you're hungry, eat."

The truth of this simple saying began to sink in. Seeing that Jala was still alive and actually seeming to enjoy herself, Milo stepped forward to take his first tentative bite. It was tart. Having eaten two blackberries the night before, Milo was already prepared for the tartness. What caught him off guard was that the tartness was soon followed by a beautiful sweetness that almost reminded him of his mother's milk. Every bite tasted a little sweeter than the one that came before it, and Milo soon found himself gulping down raspberries as fast as he could shake them off the branches.

Once the shock wore off, Azaza and Jack joined them and soon realized that they actually enjoyed the taste. Genny, after spitting out the first two berries, was eventually able to choke down a bite or two. An hour later four of the five wolves were full and all of them had enough energy to resume their lessons. They were pouncing and leaping, bounding and stalking all over the raspberry patch until in the end they were all quite covered in splotches of pink.

Full of energy as they were, it took the group no time at all to make it back to the rendezvous to share their good news. Dace was too tired to make even the short journey to the raspberry fields. So with Milo and Jack promising to bring Dace a whole bush of berries when they returned, the young wolf pack set off behind their alpha male to eat their first vegetarian feast.

Jala stayed behind with Dace. The raspberries were delicious and Jala certainly could have eaten more of them, but a little voice in her head kept saying, “People are more important than food, Jala,” over and over again in her mind. Dace was not exactly a person, but Jala thought she was close enough for it to count.

Jala curled up next to Dace on a bed of pine needles, nestling into Dace’s jet black fur. The few silver hairs reminded Jala of the first stars appearing in the night sky. It was almost evening, and soon the real stars would be appearing in the sky. Jala wondered if the great dog would be among them.

"You will."

The words startled Jala out of her day dream. "I won't," Jala said dreamily. "This is my pack now. My place is here."

"You will," Dace repeated. "Your pack is out there, beyond the stars. If you stay here you will need to take your place as alpha female, and although I suspect you and Milo would make a handsome couple, you are both too young to mate."

Mate? Mate! Jala felt so stupid. Of course the alpha pair mated. They mated in the fall and the female birthed cubs in the winter. Jala had seen her mother gritting her teeth and breathing against the pain when her little brother was about to be born. She had no desire to go through that anytime soon and maybe not ever.

“But the alpha female has other jobs, too, right? Like teaching the cubs to hunt and protecting them from predators.”

“I think our alpha male is stepping into that role quite nicely, don’t you?”

Jala had to admit that he was. Now that the cubs weren’t so hungry they would learn very quickly. Without the frenzy of hunger telling them to jump at the first chance, Azaza, Genny, and Jack would probably actually catch the rabbit the next time they cornered one. They would all be fat and ready for winter in no time.

Still, being a wolf was amazing. Jala didn't want to give it up so quickly. "You said you needed me to help strengthen the pack come spring. Please let me stay," she whimpered.

"Dear little cub, that is not up to me. And I think you would feel differently if you knew how devastated your mother would be to be without you."

Dace was right, of course. Her mother would be inconsolable. Then Jala began to think of home and its human comforts. Her bed. Her toys. Her father's silly faces. Her mother's arms. As much fun as it was to be a wolf, Jala realized that she had never thought about how much it meant to her to listen to a story and be kissed once, twice, and then twice more on each cheek before settling into bed. It was time. Jala was ready to go home.

"How do I get there? How do I get home?"

"It's simple, my dear. You only have to wake up."

Chapter 9

Home

Jala had decided to go for one final run and was mid-leap when her mother shook her awake. She could still feel the breeze ruffling her fur as her forelegs and hind legs stretched out in opposite directions in the endless stream of wolf-flight.

"You were tired, weren't you baby?" Her mother scooped her up and cradled her, rocking her a little the way she often did. Jala could feel her mother's hand smoothing down the wild hairs at the front of her head. She closed her eyes and let herself be enveloped in her mother's love.

"Breakfast is ready. I made cream of wheat with cinnamon and apples. And after breakfast maybe you could help me make the bean pies? Thanksgiving is tomorrow, you know, and we've got a lot to do to get ready."

Jala's mother paused, taking in this moment of holding her little girl rather than rushing off to work or chores as she so often did.

"Jala, do you know that you are EXACTLY

the daughter that I asked for?" Jala did know. Her mother had been telling her this for as long as she could remember and it felt wonderful every time.

"You're clever and kind and love to read, just like I asked."

This next part was Jala's favorite.

"Actually, you're even more than I asked for because I didn't even ask for my daughter to be beautiful, but you are! Smart, kind, AND beautiful? Jala, you are amazing and I'm so glad you're mine."

Jala looked up at her mother and hugged her in response. This really was where she belonged and in that moment her life had never felt so perfect.

Her mother's hands, which had been smoothing her hair so gently, suddenly switched to tugging. Jala was flooded by a momentary panic. She prayed that her mother wasn't going to ruin this perfect moment by saying that Jala needed to get her hair combed. She didn't. What Jala's mother said instead was, "Pine needles? I'm used to pulling rubber mulch out of your hair, Jala. But pine needles? Are there even any pine trees near your school?"

Jala just smiled at her mother and didn't say a word. She didn't have to. Her mother was magical. She knew.

About the Author

Marti Dumas is a mama who spends most of her time doing mama things. You know-- feeding ducks in parks, constructing Halloween costumes, facilitating heated negotiations, reading aloud, throwing raw vegetables on a plate and calling it dinner, and shouting, "watch out!" whenever there are dog piles on the walk to school. Sometimes she writes, but only very occasionally and in the early morning.

There are more stories lurking about in her brain, and her beloved son is most impatient that at least one of them should be about him. Only time will tell.